To Philip, Love,

To Philip, Love,

MERLION ARTS LIBRARY

STORIES
IN ART

Written by Helen Williams

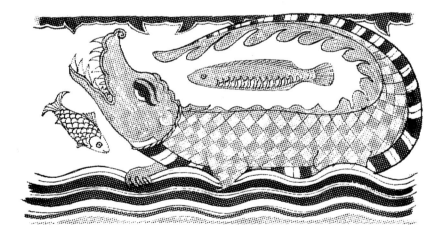

Merlion Publishing

Copyright © 1991 Merlion Publishing Ltd.
First published 1991 by
Merlion Publishing Ltd
2 Bellinger Close
Greenways Business Park
Chippenham
Wiltshire SN15 1BN
UK

3rd printing 1993

Design: Paul Fielder
Series Editor: Charlotte Ryrie

Printed in Great Britain by BPCC Paulton Books

ISBN 1 85737 055 4

Cover artwork by Richard Berridge and Gwen and Shirley Tourret
(B L Kearley Ltd); photography by Mike Stannard.

Artwork on pages 23, 25, 27, 28–29, 31, 35, 37, 38–39 by Paul
Fielder; pages 5, 7, 9, 13 21 by Andrew Midgley and pages 11, 17, 19,
33 by Edward Russell.

Photographs on pages 23, 25, 27, 28–29, 31, 34, 35, 37, 42–43 by
Mike Stannard.

✦
CONTENTS

An unknown American artist painted 'Moses Marcy in a Landscape'.

Clues in a picture

There is a story behind every picture you see. Artists use their skills to tell us either about themselves or their subjects in pictures. Some paintings tell their stories in unusual ways that may seem hard to understand. But other paintings are full of clues from the painter to help us understand them.

About the man

This American painting tells us all about a man's life. It is a picture of an American mill owner called Moses Marcy who lived in the 1700s. Let's look at its details to see what kind of man Moses Marcy was. There is a pipe on the table next to him. So we know that Moses Marcy liked to smoke tobacco.

About his work

What can we find out about Moses Marcy's life? The large sailing ship is a clue to his work. Flour from the mill may have been sent to distant places by ship. We can see that Moses Marcy had a grand house, so he was obviously a successful man. Do you think that the book on the table is his accounts book?

Clues about you

How would you tell people about your life in a picture? Write down a list of everything that is important to you.

What do you like best to eat? Where do you live? Do you like sunny days? Do you like to run fast? Do you like reading, cycling or climbing trees?

When you have made a list, take a large sheet of white paper, a pencil and your paints. Sketch a picture which includes everything on your list. Try to make the most attractive arrangement, or composition, you can. Then paint your picture. Use bright colours to make it lively and interesting.

A life story

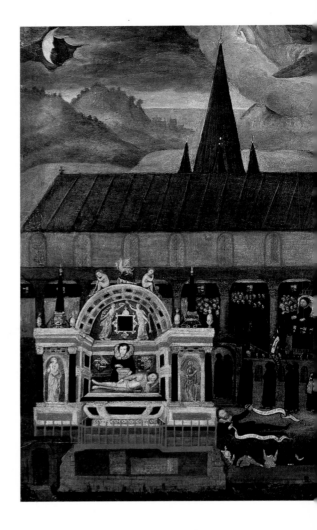

We have seen how places and objects in a painting can be clues to a person's life. Details like the clothes they wear are clues which can tell us when and where they lived. Occasionally, an artist decides to record so many details in a painting that there is no need for clues. This unusual picture includes every important thing that happened to Sir Henry Unton, a wealthy Englishman who lived in the 1500s.

A busy life

In the middle of the painting is a portrait of Sir Henry Unton. The rest of the picture tells the story of his life. The story starts in the bottom right-hand corner with Henry as a baby. Above this scene is a simple view of the city of Oxford, a university town. If you look carefully you can see a young man studying in a room. This is Sir Henry Unton as a student.

Other countries

After studying at Oxford, Sir Henry Unton travelled to other countries. In the top right of the painting, you can see him in France, Italy, and the Low Countries. This is the old name for modern-day Holland, Belgium and Luxembourg. During this part of his life, Sir Henry was an important soldier. You can see him standing outside a tent, preparing for battle.

Sir Henry Unton returned to England to live the life of a rich country gentleman. You can see him at home in his splendid house where musicians are playing and people are feasting. In the top of this section, Sir Henry is sitting in his study, but he is also at the head of the dining table. On the left, he is performing with other musicians, and below that he is speaking with a group of educated men. Why do you think he is shown doing so many things at one time?

Bad luck in France

Sir Henry returned to France, but he was badly hurt when he fell from his horse. He caught a fever and died.

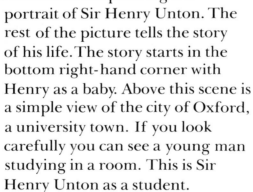

All this is recorded in the centre of the picture, at the top. Below the death scene, you can see the ship with black sails that took his body back to England. Across the bottom of the painting is a grand funeral procession leading to the church where Sir Henry was buried. Can you see the huge monument that was built in his memory?

A cartoon story of your life

Try making a cartoon to show all the most important things that have happened to you. Start with your birth, and include pictures of yourself at home, at school and playing with friends. Try to join the events together so that it is easy to follow the story.

An unknown English artist painted this picture of Sir Henry Unton.

The story of a year

'January' is one of a series of paintings called 'Les Très Riches Heures du Duc de Berry'.

Do you have a calendar in your home? If you do, it probably has a different picture for each month of the year. The first calendars came from Europe in the 1400s. At that time, most art in Europe was about the Christian religion. Painters were asked to paint pictures to decorate churches, or to tell religious stories. A calendar was part of a prayer book and was known as a Book of Hours. It had a picture for each month or season of the year.

January

This lively picture comes from a French calendar painted for a rich nobleman. The nobleman himself, dressed in blue robes and a fur hat, is sitting at a table spread with delicious food. He is celebrating the coming of the new year with his guests. Outside, knights are fighting a battle and there is a great castle in the distance. The sky is painted in vivid blues and golds. The two symbols in the sky come from a group of twelve signs known as the Zodiac.

October

The other painting is from the same French calendar. It shows farmers sowing corn in fields in front of a magnificent castle. Do you think this is the nobleman's castle? The farmers are busy in the front field but the back one is already sown. It has been covered in nets to stop birds eating the seeds.

These paintings were painted by three Dutch brothers, the Limbourg brothers. The pictures are known as 'Les Très Riches Heures du Duc de Berry'. The Limbourg brothers looked through magnifying glasses to paint the tiny details of each picture.

A special time of year

Is there a special time during the year when you have a celebration? It could be a feast day or a parade. Try to copy the shape and style of the paintings on these pages in a picture of your favourite time of year.

Buildings should go in the background. If you include a group of people paint them near the front of your picture. Use your brightest colours for everybody's clothes, and make the sky a brilliant blue. Draw a semi-circle at the top of your painting and write the name and date of the festival you have drawn inside it in careful handwriting.

'October' is another painting from this series, whose title means 'The Very Rich Hours of the Duke of Berry'.

Celebrations

Styles of painting are always changing. New ideas become popular and old ideas go out of fashion. If you compare an ancient painting with a modern one, they may have little in common. But celebrations have been popular subjects for paintings throughout the ages. Both the paintings on these pages celebrate the birth of a baby.

Noise and colour

This is a painting of a joyful occasion. A peacock is screeching on the roof, a crowd is bustling outside the palace walls, and musicians are crashing cymbals, banging drums and playing trumpets. We can almost hear the noise! There is great excitement because a royal baby has been born.

The picture celebrates the birth of a son to Akbar, a Mughal emperor, who ruled India about 400 years ago. Every detail about the event has been recorded. Each time you look at the picture you will probably find something that you missed before. The complicated patterns and clear, warm colours add to the feeling of excitement.

A feast

The other picture also shows a noisy celebration. The Dutch artist, Jan Steen, has painted a comfortable room where friends and relations crowd around a proud father holding his new-born baby. Food is being prepared for a feast.

This Mughal miniature is called 'Rejoicing at the Birth of Prince Salim'.

Everybody seems to be talking at once! The colours are much softer than those in the Mughal painting. They show the relaxed and happy mood of the event.

A special event

Try to copy the Mughal style of painting in your own picture of a special event. Choose a birthday or a festival. Use a piece of white paper or card no larger than 10 centimetres square. Begin by making a detailed pencil drawing. Put the most important things in the middle of the picture.

'The Christening Feast' was painted by the Dutch artist, Jan Steen.

Make up some decorative patterns and use them to fill in the edges. If you include people, their faces don't have to be very life-like, but do make their clothes as realistic as you can. Colour your picture carefully with bright colours. Take lots of time over your painting. Mughal artists often took months to complete one picture!

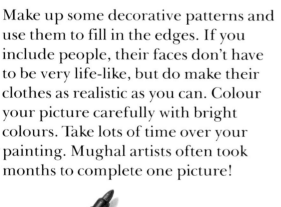

Everyday events

The Japanese artist, Kitagawa Utamaro, painted 'Child Upsetting a Goldfish Bowl'.

You have just looked at two detailed pictures telling simple stories. Sometimes pictures seem to be showing a simple event, but can tell us quite complicated stories.

A Japanese child

When Japanese prints and paintings were first seen around the world, people were surprised at how ordinary some of the scenes were. Japanese artists realized that paintings did not have to show grand scenes to be interesting. They painted everyday events as they saw them.

This coloured print shows a woman asleep as her child plays beside her. But it tells us much more. Look at the way the woman is sleeping. It looks as though she has fallen asleep because her restless son has completely worn her out! While she sleeps, he has tipped over the large, green goldfish bowl. For a few moments, he is completely happy gazing at the water splashing onto the floor. The fish are nowhere to be seen! What do you think his mother will say when she wakes up?

A fishing trip

The picture on the opposite page, by the Swedish artist Carl Larsson, shows a family fishing for crayfish. It is obviously not the first time they have been on a trip like this. Everything is well organized! Although they are having a picnic, there is even a table, beautifully spread with china plates and glasses. Can you see the huge pile of crayfish ready to eat? All the members of the family are busy except for one girl, who is sitting waiting patiently for her food.

Carl Larsson painted hundreds of pictures of his family enjoying their country life. If we look at the detail in his simple pictures, we can find out all about life in Sweden at the end of the 1800s. Each of his pictures is like a single photograph from a long movie. They are all part of a larger story.

A common event

When you are at home you probably eat a meal sitting with your family. This won't seem very interesting to you, because you are used to it. But pretend you are a stranger looking at the scene in 100 years' time. You would probably be fascinated by every detail!

What does the room where you eat look like? Do you have shelves on the walls? What do you sit on? What sort of things do you eat? Include all these details in your picture. Try to draw everything to the right scale, and use realistic colours. Perhaps someone will find your picture 100 years from now!

'Crayfishing' was painted by the Swedish artist, Carl Larsson.

Travelling tales

Most people today take travel for granted. Even if we have never travelled away from our own country, we have probably seen pictures and films of distant places. But before machines like trains were invented, travelling was much more difficult.

This English picture was painted more than a 100 years ago, when train travel was a new experience. The artist, William Frith, was fascinated by the stories he saw happening around him at stations. His picture is full of interesting details of travellers at a London station.

A bride and a soldier

A large collection of people are milling around on the busy station platform.

'The Railway Station' was painted by the English artist, William Powell Frith.

Can you see the girls saying goodbye to the bride in her wedding dress? A mother is kissing her young son goodbye while an older boy stands by. The older boy wants nothing to do with the scene! A soldier in a splendid red uniform is joyfully lifting his baby up into the air. Do you think he has just come home on the train? He is delighted to see his child again!

Frith wanted to paint everything that was happening at the station. He wanted to record the stories of each group of people as he saw them. He took over a year and a half to complete the painting.

The English artist, JMW Turner painted 'Rain, Steam and Speed'.

Speed

The English artist, JMW Turner, painted a train in a totally different style. You would hardly think that he was painting at the same time as Frith, and in the same country! Turner was fascinated by light and colour. He wanted to capture the speed of a train dashing across a bridge. The steam from the engine hides the places on either side as the train rushes past.

There is a story behind this painting. A young woman at the time was travelling on a train in England in 1844, when she was amazed to see the man opposite her take off his hat and lean out of the window. He leaned out for several minutes, even though it was raining hard and the train was going at full speed. The man was Turner. This dramatic painting was the result of his first-hand experience of the train's speed.

Creatures from travellers' stories

Before the invention of modern methods of transport like trains, people travelled the world by boat. These early explorers returned home with stories about the wonderful things they saw.

'The Whale' comes from the Ashmole Bestiary.

But some of their descriptions were so amazing that they were hard to believe. It must have been tempting for the travellers to exaggerate their adventures. Or perhaps the memories of their experiences seemed more marvellous when they reached home!

Bestiaries

Some explorers wrote books describing strange foreign animals that they had seen. The books were called bestiaries. They contained descriptions and drawings of the creatures. The pictures were often drawn by an artist, from a traveller's description. Can you imagine how notes about an unusual animal could become an even stranger picture?

The first place in each bestiary was usually given to the lion. Descriptions of many real and imagined animals followed. Tired eagles were said to get their strength back by flying near the hot sun, then plunging themselves three times into a fountain.

The whale

The sight of a whale confused and frightened many early sailors. A whale resting near the surface of the sea looked so large that some sailors thought it was an island. This painting from an English bestiary records how striking the sight of a whale must have been. It seems to have an enormous number of fins and tails, and its face looks almost human.

The unicorn

This beautiful French tapestry shows an extraordinary beast called a unicorn. A unicorn is an imaginary animal which appears in tales from many countries. It has the head and body of a horse, the legs of a deer and the tail of a lion. Most importantly, it has a single horn in the middle of its forehead. People think that the idea of the unicorn comes from travellers' tales about the rhinoceros!

This French tapestry is called 'Lady and the Unicorn with Lion, Animals and Flowers'.

Drawing a fantastic animal

Ask a friend to describe a strange animal to you. Then take some paper and coloured crayons, and try to make a drawing from their description.

Here is a description of an unusual creature. It has the head of a lizard but the body of a leopard. Its huge eyes are the blue of the deep sea. There are hooves on its back feet but four claws on each front foot. It strides along on its back legs, holding its tail high over its back. Here is a picture of the creature. Would you have drawn it like this?

Stories about dragons

How would you paint a picture of a creature you could never see? Dragons are imaginary creatures, which appear in stories and pictures all over the world. In the East, dragons are seen as powerful creatures who can bring great good fortune as well as bad luck. In Europe, dragons were always described in stories as wicked creatures.

This Chinese embroidered robe was made in the 1800s.

Chinese dragons

According to Chinese stories, the dragon is a magnificent and sacred beast. One description gives it a mane like a lion, horns above its eyes, fins like a fish and a scaly body. It breathes out fire and a pearl rests in the middle of the flames. This dragon can cause rain, wind and storms when it is angry.

Chinese dragons can also bring good fortune. If you look up at the sky during a heavy rainstorm you may catch a glimpse of a dragon. But you can never see the whole of it because it has such a long tail. If you do see the dragon, you will have a long life and great riches. Dragons frequently appear on Chinese porcelain and fabrics, as well as on paintings and scrolls. This marvellous dragon robe was made about 100 years ago for a lady in the Chinese imperial court.

European dragons

The dragon in European stories is always seen as an evil monster. It lives in a dark cave and captures people to eat. A dragon can only be killed if it is blinded. Stories tell us about a brave nobleman who kills the dragon and rescues a captured girl. In most stories, the dragon is killed by a hero called Saint George. You can see Saint George fighting the dragon in this painting by the Italian artist, Paolo Uccello.

'Saint George and the Dragon' was painted by the Italian artist, Paolo Uccello.

Allegories

A picture like Uccello's is sometimes called an allegory. This means that each character in the story has a special meaning. In European stories, the dragon stands for everything that is evil. The girl represents gentleness and innocence. And the fine and noble hero who rescues her is a sign of all that is good. The allegories describe how goodness defeats wickedness through the story of the dragon, the hero and the girl.

Good and bad

Paint a picture showing a dragon that is bad, and one that is good. Which colours would you use for a frightening dragon? Which colours would show gentleness?

A well-known myth

The Flemish artist, Pieter Brueghel, painted 'The Fall of Icarus'.

Some stories about imaginary people or animals are well known in many countries. These stories are called myths. Many of the myths we know today come from Ancient Greek stories.

Daedalus and Icarus

One Ancient Greek myth tells the story of a man called Daedalus and his son Icarus. A Greek king called Minos quarrelled with Daedalus and imprisoned him and his son. Daedalus planned a clever escape. He made two pairs of wings out of feathers held together with wax so that they could fly away. He told Icarus not to fly too near the sun as they escaped over the sea. But Icarus didn't listen. He enjoyed flying so much that he flew higher. Can you guess what happened?

The sun melted the wax, the feathers came unstuck, and Icarus fell out of the sky. If you look carefully at the painting on this page, you can see Icarus falling into the sea.

Many different artists have painted pictures of this myth. This painting is by the Flemish artist, Pieter Brueghel. He doesn't make the story look very exciting! No one seems to be taking much notice of the extraordinary things which are happening. Can you see Icarus' tiny legs? Does it look as though anyone else has noticed them? Brueghel has turned a serious tale into a picture to make us laugh. The little fat legs look quite ridiculous splashing in the sea!

Guessing about the painting

Do the farmers in this painting look at all modern? Have you ever seen a sailing ship like the one here? When you look at a new painting, spend a few moments guessing when it might have been painted. Sometimes you can tell from the way it is painted. Sometimes you can guess because of the clothes people are wearing. This picture was painted in about 1560.

A puzzle of paths

When king Minos imprisoned Daedalus and Icarus, he held them captive inside a maze. A maze is a structure made of a complicated pattern of walls, hedges or paths. There is a picture of a maze on this page. Can you trace a way around the puzzle to reach the centre? You can see mazes in parks and gardens today.

Stories about animals

The Italian artist, Jacopo Bassano, painted 'Animals Entering the Ark'.

Real as well as imaginary animals have been painted and drawn since earliest times. If you look through this book, you will find animals creeping, running or flying on many of the pages! The two pictures on these pages tell stories about large groups of animals.

An ancient story

The Italian artist, Jacopo Bassano, has painted an ancient story. An old man called Noah was warned that there was going to be a great flood that

would cover the whole earth. He was told to build a boat to carry one pair of every living creature to save them from drowning. Here, we see Noah and his family shepherding a huge group of animals onto the boat.

Can you recognize all the animals? Bassano painted this picture before 1600. It is not likely that he would have been able to travel to other countries to see wild animals. You may be able to tell which animals he had seen in real life, and which he had only heard about.

A simple style

This picture was painted about 250 years later by an American, Edward Hicks. Hicks worked as a signwriter and he painted in his spare time. His painting illustrates the words of an old story which describes a peaceful world. A lion is eating straw next to an ox, a bear feeds next to a cow and a wolf is lying down next to a lamb. Would this happen in real life? Hicks painted more than 80 versions of this story!

Unlikely friends

Make a cut-out picture, or collage, of a group of animals who might be unlikely friends! You can cut animal shapes out of paper or material, or cut animal pictures out of old magazines. Arrange your animals to make a pleasing picture.

Then glue the shapes onto a piece of white card. Can you think of a title for your collage?

The American artist, Edward Hicks, painted 'The Peaceable Kingdom'.

This crocodile is part of a storytelling scroll from Bengal, in India.

'Gazi Riding on a Tiger' follows the crocodile picture on the scroll.

Storytelling scrolls

Before movies and television were invented, people told each other stories. Storytellers were important people. In some countries, storytellers carried long scroll pictures with them to help them tell their stories. Their pictures were like the very first movies.

An Indian Scroll

In the 1800s, wandering storytellers were common throughout India. These bright pictures are from a fine scroll from Bengal. As the scroll was slowly unfolded, its pictures told the story of the travels of an important holy man.

The scroll is 13 metres long and has 57 separate paintings of different sizes. Lions, tigers, cows and elephants all appear on the scroll. None of the animals look at all fierce. These pictures show a crocodile who was a friend of the holy man. The holy man is also shown riding on a tiger's back. Can you see what he is carrying?

Your own scroll

Think of an exciting story that you have read or heard. Then paint a series of pictures to illustrate it. If you can, paint the pictures on the back of a roll of wallpaper. Or join several sheets of paper together.

Each picture is an important part of the whole story. If the story is dramatic, use colours to match the mood. If there are particular people in the story, try to make them the same in each scene so they can be easily recognized. If the story is amusing, try to put things in your picture that will make people laugh. You may like to work on your scroll with a friend.

When you have finished the main scenes, decorate the edges with brightly coloured patterns. Then use your scroll to tell your friends the story. Have you read a description of the story on the scroll below elsewhere in this book?

Unfolding history

'Harold's Oath to William' is a scene from the Bayeux Tapestry.

Tales of dramatic events like battles are passed down through the ages as exciting stories. Artists often choose well-known historical stories as subjects for pictures. This historical story was sewn or embroidered with needles and different coloured threads. This embroidered picture is known as the Bayeux Tapestry. It is 70 metres long and 50 centimetres high. It was made by a group of women about 900 years ago, and tells the story of the French defeating the English in a battle.

Lively pictures

The embroidery is full of life and humour. The part of the story shown above tells how the King of England, King Harold, promises to be loyal to Duke William of Normandy. King Harold looks very miserable.

In the next scene, Harold is returning to England in a longboat. Can you see the man on the balcony looking to see if Harold's ship is near? It is easy to laugh at the simple way the people are shown, but the result is an enjoyable story.

This scene from the Bayeux Tapestry is 'Harold's Return to England'.

A simple moving picture

The Bayeux Tapestry covers the walls of a large room in a special museum in Bayeux, France. When you walk around the room you see the story move quickly from one event to the next. It is almost as if some of the figures are moving!

You can make your own moving picture. Draw the side-view of a simple figure onto the lower right-hand corner of the first page of a notebook. Turn the page, and draw the figure again, changing its position so that it is beginning to walk.

Repeat the process on the next few pages. Copy the figures at the top of this page if you have difficulty drawing your own. Then slowly flick through the pages. Your figure should look as though it is walking.

Sculptures that tell stories

Some artists cut shapes and figures out of stone, wood or clay. The solid forms they create are called sculptures. It can take a long time to carve a sculpture, but it is a dramatic way to tell a tale.

Chinese army

Early in the 20th century, some Chinese villagers were digging a well. They were surprised to uncover a life-size pottery figure of a soldier. Can you imagine their astonishment when thousands more figures were uncovered? The figures were all made from a reddish clay called terracotta. They had been buried for more than 2,000 years in the tomb of the first Chinese emperor.

The emperor was a powerful warrior who wanted to be buried with statues of his entire army. The terracotta figures are all life-size. Sculptures of warriors and horses were buried with wooden chariots and real weapons. They were arranged in special positions to tell the story of one of the emperor's battles. No two soldiers are alike.

A storytelling frieze

The sculpture at the top of the next page was carved from a type of stone called alabaster in a palace in Assyria, which is now part of Iraq. The sculpture was made to tell the story of the great battles fought by an Assyrian king called Ashurnasirpal. It forms a long narrow border all round the main rooms in the palace. A border like this is called a frieze.

The Terracotta Warriors come from Xian, in China.

'Soldiers Swimming a Moat to Escape King Ashumasirpal' was part of a long Assyrian frieze.

In this small scene, three soldiers are trying to escape from their enemies. They must cross a swirling moat to reach safety. One of them has an arrow in his shoulder and another arrow in his side. The other two soldiers are floating on sheepskins full of air because they cannot swim. Can you see them blowing more air into the skins?

Making a frieze

You can make an interesting frieze using modelling clay. First roll out a thin rectangle of clay to make your background. Now decide what kind of figures you will have on your frieze. Perhaps you could try making sculptures of your friends.

Ask an adult to help you cut out your shapes with a knife. Use different colours for each part of your figures. Remember that you can use the end of the knife to make patterns in the clay. Look at the picture to see how to make patterns which look like hair.

Stories on walls

This is a detail from a large mural called 'The Making of Gold and Mosaic Jewellery' by the Mexican artist, Diego Rivera.

The first known pictures were scratched or painted on walls. These pictures were used to pass on historical stories and information. Modern artists sometimes paint huge pictures on the outside of buildings. These pictures are called murals. You may have seen a mural in a town near you.

Mexican murals

The modern Mexican artist, Diego Rivera, realised that mural painting was a powerful way to tell a story. He painted his murals in bright colours on huge city walls so that as many people as possible could see them.

Rivera's stories were about the everyday lives of the people of Mexico. This picture shows part of one of Rivera's murals. These people are all hard at work. They are making gold and silver jewellery. Rivera has painted in great detail to show us each stage of jewellery making from carving to the final decoration. Can you see the fire for melting down the gold and silver?

A Greek mural

Let's look at the other mural on this page. This colourful wall picture was painted by the Greek artist, Theophilos, at the beginning of the 1900s. It tells a simple story about milk. The people in the restaurant at the bottom of the picture are eating fresh yoghurt. The yoghurt is made from the milk of the

'We Have Yoghurt and Sheep's Milk' comes from a wall painting by the Greek artist, Theophilos.

cows and goats we can see at the top of the picture. Theophilos is describing everyday Greek life in his picture.

Painting on wet plaster

Some wall paintings are called frescoes. A fresco is made by painting directly onto the wet plaster of the surface of a wall. As the paint and plaster dry, they combine to make a coloured surface which won't rub off. This is a very old method of painting on walls.

Try fresco painting yourself. Cover a table with newspaper. Mix some plaster and flatten out a small square on the table. It is best to use a small amount of builder's plaster, as modelling plaster dries too fast. Then, with coloured chalk or pencil, quickly sketch the outlines of your pattern. Mix some strongly coloured waterbased paints and paint your picture or pattern as fast as you can. You have to finish the painting before the plaster dries!

Egyptian stories in tombs

'The Weighing of the Heart' comes from the Egyptian 'Book of the Dead of Ani'.

When a story is told in pictures instead of words, we can understand it whatever language we speak. Story pictures from Ancient Egypt have been discovered on the walls of tombs. A tomb is a building which is built to hold the body of a dead person. Many of the facts that we know about life in Ancient Egypt come from these tomb paintings.

A happy new life

The Ancient Egyptians had strong beliefs about what happened to them when they died. They believed that good people went on to a happy new life. Some stories about travels to the next life were painted on a type of paper called papyrus, and placed next to the dead person. Other stories were painted on the walls of the tombs.

A feather and a heart

This story was painted on the walls of a tomb of an Egyptian called Ani. It shows a test which the Egyptians believed a person had to pass after dying. To judge whether they had been good, their heart was weighed against a feather.

This was to get past the four blue baboons you can see in the picture below. The baboons would forgive the person for any small things they might have done wrong during their life. Then they could enter the next life through one of seven gates. As they went through the gate, they were given a cake, a loaf of bread and a jug of beer!

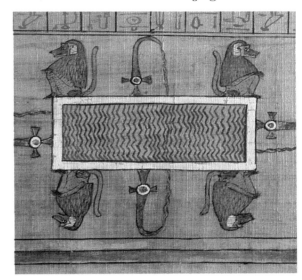

These four baboons also come from the 'Book of the Dead of Ani'.

This feather was the sign for truth. If they had been good the heart and the feather would be the same weight and they could go on to the next life.

In this picture, the scales are being checked by a god with the head of a jackal. A monster is waiting to gobble up the heart if it weighs more than the feather. The two people dressed in white are the dead man, Ani, and his wife.

The four baboons

If the dead person passed the first test, they had to give a special password.

Words in pictures

The Ancient Egyptians wrote in pictures rather than letters and words. This form of writing is called hieroglyphics. You can see some of this picture writing in the paintings. Can you read the message written in hieroglyphs on this page? Some pictures stand for whole words, others stand for letters or for parts of words.

Stories on everyday objects

Look around your home. You may have some paintings hanging on the walls. But can you see interesting pictures anywhere else? Look at the floor. Pictures are often woven on rugs and carpets. Can you also see pictures painted on cups or plates?

Decorated plates and vases

In the 1700s and 1800s, European travellers to China were impressed by the pictures they saw on beautiful old Chinese plates and vases. Some of these traditional designs were changed slightly and copied in Europe. This blue and white design came from China in the 1800s. It tells the story of a young couple in love. They were forbidden by the girl's father to marry. A kind servant helped the girl to escape with the young man. Can you see three tiny figures running across a little bridge beneath a willow tree?

For a while the couple lived safely together in the tiny house. But soon they had to escape further. They swam out to the boat, which took them to the small island. They lived there until the angry father found them. The young man was killed and the unhappy young woman set their house on fire. She died in the flames. But the couple were changed into the pair of blue birds you can see at the top of the plate. And they lived together happily forever.

This willow pattern plate is a copy of a Chinese design.

Persian carpets

This brightly patterned carpet comes from Persia. It was made at the beginning of the 1900s. Rugs are often woven with pictures or patterns which tell stories. Can you work out the story on this carpet? Perhaps it was made for the grand lady we can see in the middle of the picture. Do you think the young man is asking her to marry him?

Make a photograph frame

By making your own frame for a photograph, you can make an ordinary object tell a story. To make the frame, cut a piece of stiff backing card which is 2 centimetres longer and wider than your photograph. You also need 4 strips of white card 3 centimetres wide and the same length as the edges of your backing card.

This is a Persian picture carpet.

Stick the four strips carefully onto the edges of backing card, leaving the top edge open. You can slip your photograph in here. With a sharp pencil, draw a design which tells a story about the person in the photograph. Include the food they like to eat or their favourite sport. Colour your pictures in carefully and make the background bright and bold.

Story pictures from books

'The Foxe and the Raysyns' is a print from a wood engraving by the German artist, Anton Sorg.

Popular stories

In Ancient Greece, a wise man named Aesop made up hundreds of amusing stories about animals. All the creatures behave like humans. The ones that behave badly are always punished, and those that behave well are always rewarded. These kind of stories are called fables. Aesop's fables have been very popular in many countries for a long time.

One of the earliest illustrated books of Aesop's fables was made in the 1500s in Germany. This picture is a wood engraving from the book by Anton Sorg. Because each engraving could be printed hundreds of times, exactly the same pictures could be produced over and over again.

On every page in this book you can look at beautiful pictures in different colours. Thousands of other people will be able to look at other copies of the same book. But this has not always been possible. The earliest books were all handpainted. Each book took so long to paint that usually only one copy was made. In the 1400s, new printing methods meant that many copies of the same picture could be printed at the same time.

An angry fox

The sly fox appears in many of Aesop's fables. In the story picture above, the fox was hungry so he spent a long time trying to reach the delicious grapes above him. Eventually, the angry fox gave up. Aesop told the story to tell us that we can't always get what we want, and that we often don't need it anyway!

A disappointed cockerel

This picture is by the Japanese artist, Kano Tomonobu. It illustrates a French version of one of Aesop's fables. Japanese artists are famous for their fine wood engravings. This engraving was made in 1894, but it copies the style of Japanese prints from the 1600s.

The story shows a cockerel scratching in the farmyard. Among the stones and dirt he finds a precious jewel. Instead of being pleased, the cockerel is disappointed. He was only interested in food and thought the jewel was no use to him. Aesop's fable tells us to be happy with what we are given!

String prints

Make a print to decorate several sheets of paper with the same image. Cover some short lengths of fine string with glue. Then stick them onto one side of a block of wood, curling them round to make the shape you want. For your first try, make the shape of the first letter of your name, and wind a leaf or plant shape around the letter.

When the glue is dry, paint over the surface of the wood block. The paint will stick onto the raised bits of string.

Press the painted surface onto paper to make a clear print. Why not use your paper to write letters to all your friends.

'The Cockerel and the Pearl' was painted by the Japanese artist, Kano Tomonobu.

Unusual stories

You don't have to understand a story completely before you can enjoy it. Some pictures have been painted from stories which are long forgotten. Other paintings tell stories in such an unusual way that we can only guess what they are about.

'The Lion and the Antelope Playing Senet' comes from an Ancient Egyptian storytelling scroll.

Animal people

This picture makes us smile because two animals are acting like human beings. They are sitting on stools playing a board game similar to chess or draughts. The lion looks as though he is wearing glasses. But this is most unlikely because he was painted over 3,000 years ago, long before glasses were invented!

The picture is part of a long Egyptian storytelling scroll where every animal is shown as if it is a real person. We no longer know what stories the pictures originally told.

Dream-like images

Many paintings by the Swiss artist, Paul Klee, show a strange world that is hard to understand. Klee's pictures look like the doodles you might make along the edge of a notebook! It can be hard to remember that Klee was a trained artist who chose to paint in this way.

Klee's fishtank painting might be a scene from an extraordinary dream. In the centre of the picture there is a clock in a net. There are plants, vases of flowers and strange figures. The figure on the right has both sides of her face showing at once. In spite of all this disorder, the fish swim quietly around in their underwater world. They don't seem at all disturbed.

We can be sure that Klee included all the objects here for a reason. See if you can

work out a story that fits the images in the painting. It doesn't matter that your story might be different from the one Klee had in mind.

The Swiss painter, Paul Klee, painted 'Magic Fish'.

Your special picture

Think of some things that are special to you. Or something that you like doing, such as cycling or playing football. You may have a favourite animal, or particularly like one type of plant or flower. How would you show these special things in a painting?

Look at the way Klee has used shapes and colours to make a pattern on paper. Sketch the objects you have chosen on a large piece of white paper. Make sure that you make a pleasing arrangement. When you are happy with the design of your picture, paint it in your favourite colours. Does your picture look anything like Klee's painting?

The story of a painter's life

'Twelve Sunflowers in a Vase' is one of Vincent van Gogh's most famous paintings.

We have looked at the way artists use their pictures to tell stories. We can also use paintings to tell the story of an artist's life. An artist's style often changes several times. These changes in style can tell us about the artist.

Vincent van Gogh

The Dutch artist, Vincent van Gogh, painted over 800 paintings during the last 10 years of his life. They were not appreciated at all when he painted them. Yet they are so popular now that they are bought and sold for huge sums of money. In the 1980s, this picture of sunflowers was sold for so much money that it became the most expensive painting in the world.

Dark and sad

Before he started to paint, van Gogh studied the Christian religion, and spent several years preaching in Belgium. He was not very well suited to this kind of life. He was so unhappy that he fell ill. His brother Theo encouraged him to take up painting. Van Gogh painted the farmers and miners and people he lived with in Belgium. The pictures he painted at this time were dark and sad.

'The Potato Eaters' is an early painting by Vincent van Gogh.

'Seascape at Sainte-Marie' is a view of the Mediterranean Sea by Vincent van Gogh.

Sunshine and colour

In 1886, van Gogh went to Paris to visit his brother. While he was in Paris he saw the colourful pictures of a group of painters called the Impressionists. He was excited by the brightness and joy in these paintings. As a result, his style changed. He moved to southern France in 1888. This picture of the sea is typical of his paintings from this time. It is full of colour and activity.

Unwell and unhappy

But van Gogh was still not happy. In 1889, after a quarrel with the French painter, Paul Gauguin, van Gogh took a razor and cut off part of his own right ear. Soon after, he became seriously ill. In 1890, van Gogh killed himself.

What the pictures tell us

When you know a little about Vincent van Gogh's life, you can look at his pictures differently. Look again at the pictures on these two pages. The dark colours and heavy brushstrokes of 'The Potato Eaters' on the page opposite tell us that this picture was painted while he was living in Belgium. Can you tell when the picture of sunflowers was painted? Do you think he was happy when he painted the self-portrait on the right? It was painted shortly before he died.

'Self-portrait' was painted by Vincent van Gogh a year before he died.

Restoring paintings

Many early paintings were painted on surfaces prepared with gesso. This is a kind of boiled plaster. If the gesso has cracked under the paint, tiny holes appear in the painting. These can fill with dirt. Restorers use fine tools to pick the dirt out of every tiny hole.

Removing extra paint

People have sometimes been upset by naked figures in paintings. So they painted clothes onto the figures! Today, experts use X-ray photographs to see how a painting first looked. Then restorers remove any layers of paint that don't belong to the original painting.

Replacing the backing

Sometimes the back of a painting needs restoring. The first oil paintings were painted onto linen cloth. Over the years, the cloth weakens and eventually can no longer support the paint. Clever restorers can replace the backing, leaving the painting intact. They carefully scrape away the old cloth. Then they join the old painting to a new canvas lining with hot wax. They do this on a special heated table.

Old paintings can gradually fall into a poor condition. They become covered with dirt from the air. Paint tends to crack, and colours may fade or darken. There are specialists who know about the old methods of painting. They can bring paintings back to their original condition. We call this process restoring a painting. All restoration work takes a long time and a great deal of skill.

Varnish

Most paintings are covered with a light varnish to protect them. Varnish may turn brown and crack or blister as it ages. The first stage in restoring a painting is to remove the old varnish. To do this, skilled restorers use tiny pieces of soft material such as cotton wool, dipped in a special liquid, like alcohol. The cotton wool is rubbed gently over the surface of the painting. The alcohol dissolves the varnish and is mopped up by the cotton wool. This work must be done slowly and carefully so that the paint below the varnish is not dissolved as well.

Cleaning the painting

Once the varnish is removed the paint can be cleaned. Paintings may be in poor condition because the backing board or canvas has become damaged. Or because the varnish has cracked or become discoloured. If the backing of the painting was not prepared properly, the paint may have flaked or cracked.

Artists' biographies

A biography is the history of a person's life. These short biographies will help you to find out more about some of the artists mentioned in this book.

Jacopo Bassano (1510–1592)

The Italian painter, Jacopo Bassano, was the father of a family of painters. They all worked together in one studio. At the time, most paintings in Italy showed religious or historical stories. The Bassano family were some of the first painters to make the animals and scenery in a painting more important than the story behind the picture.

Pieter Brueghel (the Elder) (c.1525–1569)

Pieter Brueghel was born in the Netherlands. We don't know much about his life except that he visited Italy and France. He is called 'the Elder' because his son was also called Pieter. He is sometimes known as Peasant Brueghel. Brueghel actually lived in a town but most of his pictures show simple village people at work and play. Some of his paintings are funny, and most are full of energy. They leave a vivid record of peasant life in the 1500s.

Edward Hicks (1780–1849)

The American artist, Edward Hicks, was a signpainter by trade. He was a deeply Christian man, and a part-time preacher. Painting was his hobby, and he painted hundreds of simple pictures. These paintings illustrate his beliefs about the importance of peace in the world. There were many painters like Hicks in America in the 1700s and 1800s. They are known as folk artists, or naive painters. They were artists who had never studied art. They all painted in a simple style.

Paul Klee (1879–1940)

Paul Klee was a Swiss painter who described his paintings as "taking a line for a walk". His pictures are painted in a strange, simple style. He loved all kinds of art as a child, and was very good at playing the violin. He was a brilliant art teacher and taught for many years at the German Bauhaus. This was a famous college that tried to show how art was important in everyday life. Klee was one of a group of artists who were known as The Blue Rider group.

The Limbourg brothers (died c.1416)

Jean, Herman and Pol de Limbourg came from the Netherlands. They were famous as brilliant illustrators. As teenagers they worked for a goldsmith in Paris. This was important training for their work on detailed miniature paintings. But this work for a rich man also caused some trouble. At one time the brothers were imprisoned by a greedy nobleman in Brussels until a ransom was paid to set them free. The Limbourgs were employed by rich French noblemen. It is believed that they died from an outbreak of the plague in about 1415.

Jan Steen (1626–1679)

The Dutch painter, Jan Steen, was born in Leiden in Holland. He is well known as a painter of humorous, everyday scenes. His crowded colourful pictures often show people of all ages laughing, eating or dancing. Some of the people he painted were figures from the Dutch popular theatre of the time. Steen also painted works based on proverbs and stories from the Christian religion.

was the most important thing in Uccello's life. His fellow artists thought that he was completely mad!

Kitagawa Utamaro (1753–1806)

Kitagawa Utamaro was a leading Japanese printmaker. At the start of his career in Tokyo, he concentrated on nature studies and published many illustrated books. In about 1791, he turned to making portraits of beautiful women. He often painted women from the waist up, to capture their elegant hands, faces and hairstyles.

Paolo Uccello (1396–1475)

Paolo Uccello was an Italian painter who lived for a long time but painted very little. Uccello was fascinated with new ideas about space and perspective. He was one of the first painters to try to make his figures look solid. As a result, all his paintings of horses look like carved toy horses rather than real creatures. It is said that perspective

Index

The publishers would like to thank the following for permission to reproduce these works of art:

'Lady and the Unicorn with Lion, Animals and Flowers', French tapestry; 'We have Yoghurt and Sheep's Milk' by Theophilos, 1873-1934, both by courtesy of the Ancient Art & Architecture Collection, London, UK. 'The Whale' from the Ashmole Bestiary, by courtesy of the Bodleian Library, Oxford, UK. 'Crayfishing' by Carl Larsson, 1855-1919, in the National Museum, Stockholm, Sweden; 'The Railway Station' by William Powell Frith, 1819-1909, in the Royal Holloway and Bedford New College, Egham, Surrey, UK; 'Rain, Steam and Speed' by JMW Turner, 1775-1851, in the National Gallery, London, UK; 'Saint George and the Dragon' by Paolo Uccello, 1397-1475, in the National Gallery, London, UK; 'Fall of Icarus' by Pieter Brueghel the Elder, c.1515-1569, in the Musées Royaux des Beaux-Arts de Belgique, Brussels, Belgium; 'Animals Entering the Ark' by Jacopo Bassano, 1510-1592, in the Prado, Madrid, Spain; 'The Peaceable Kingdom' by Edward Hicks, 1780-1849, in Philadephia Museum of Art, Pennsylvania, USA; Detail from 'The Making of Gold and Mosaic jewellery' by Diego Rivera, 1886-1957, in the National Palace, Mexico; 'Magic Fish' by Paul Klee, 1879-1940, in the Philadelphia Museum of Art, Pennsylvania, USA; 'The Potato Eaters' by Vincent van Gogh, 1853-90, in the Stedelijk Museum, Amsterdam, the Netherlands; 'Twelve Sunflowers in a Vase' by Vincent van Gogh, in the Neue Pinakothek, Munich, Germany; 'Self Portrait, 1889' by Vincent van Gogh, in the Musée Orsay, Paris, France; 'Seascape at Sainte-Marie' in the Pushkin Museum, Moscow, USSR; all by courtesy of the Bridgeman Art Library, London, UK. 'Child Upsetting a Goldfish Bowl' by Kitagawa Utamaro; 'Crocodile'; 'Gazi Riding on a Tiger'; 'Soldiers Swimming a Moat to Escape from King Ashurnasirpal', an Assyrian frieze; 'The Weighing of the Heart'; 'The Four Baboons' from the Egyptian Book of the Dead of Ani; 'The Lion and Antelope playing Senet'; all by courtesy of the Trustees of the British Museum, London, UK. 'Harold's Oath to William' and 'Harold's Return to England' from the Bayeux Tapestry, from the Collection of the Musée de Bayeux, © Michael Holford Photographs, Essex, UK. 'Rain, Steam and Speed' by JMW Turner, by courtesy of the Trustees, the National Gallery, London, UK. 'Sir Henry Unton' (artist unknown) by courtesy of the National Portrait Gallery, London, UK. 'Moses Marcy in a Landscape, overmantel panel (artist unknown), B19942/Henry E Peach, by courtesy of Old Sturbridge Village, Massachusetts, USA. 'January' and 'October' from Les Très Riches Heures du Duc de Berry', by the Limbourg brothers, in the Musée Condé, by courtesy of Photographie Giraudon, Paris, France. Terracotta Warriors from Xian, China, by courtesy of Tony Stone Photolibrary, London, UK. 'Rejoicing at the Birth of Prince Salim', Chinese Dragon Robe; Persian Carpet; 'The Foxe and the Raysyns' by Anton Sorg; 'The Cockerel and the Pearl' by Kano Tomonobu; all by courtesy of the Board of Trustees of the Victoria & Albert Museum, London, UK. 'The Christening Feast' by Jan Steen, by courtesy of the Trustees, the Wallace Collection, London, UK.

The publishers would like to give special thanks to staff at the Victoria & Albert Museum, London, and to Floyd Beckford and his colleagues at the British Museum, London.